Tied Inside Artistic Mind

Tied Inside Artistic Mind

poetry from a spiritual journey

by: dariusES

CONTENTS

Two Days.1

Internal.2

To Bear.3

Atmosphere.4

The Days You Remember

Will Never Recall You.5

One Evening in Georgia.7

Distance Means Nothing.8

Thoughts to Bury This:

To Flourish Each.9

Different Roads.10

Astonishing.12

Scaling Keys.13

The Hesitation.14

Brave It.16

Scattered.17

Breadcrumbs.18

Exposed.19

A Moment of Solace.20

Coat (Armor).21

A Watch and a King.23

Stability.24

Something to Stand On.25

Grace.26

Echo.27

Reciprocal.28

Countries.29

Music.30

The Open Letter.31

Priorities.32

So Long as You Finish.33

Invite.34

Markings of Egypt.35

Art.36

Precipitation.37

A Writer.38

Content.39

On My Way.40

Survived to Hold You.41

The Music Graduate.42

How It Is.43

To Be Honest.44

The Giant.46

The Body.47

Silly Billy.48

Short Story.49

Every Year in November.51

Encourage.52

Peanut M & M's for Mom.53

1:23 AM.54

A Notice to Rose.55

It'll Be Okay.56

Beat Never Stops.57

Lit.58

Loners Perspective.59

Vault..61

satan We're Gonna Tear your kingdom Down.62

(Un)Tied.63

(Sigh) Inside).64

(Labeled) Artistic.65

Mind (Set).66

In life there is often an experience we go through that will establish perseverance which exposes the character of the individual. As humans, the majority will endure hardships. It's the attitude during our trial by fire that we must try and perfect. In truth an attribute that was hard for me to obtain was patience. I feel it is a quality which can only be perfected by God. The more the difficult times ensued, the more I learned to handle them with grace. I am still far from it, but I've learned how to better approach it. Writing has been a beautiful outlet for me throughout life. This craft brings a serenity that overshadows any disheartening days I have seen in my existence. It is my peace I will always run to in life. To share, to grow, to smile, even to mourn. A true writer will use what life brings, the good with the bad.

This Book is Dedicated to Ms. Simi

For always pouring good into my spirit

TWO DAYS

As the water knew to keep the earth growing

Like the wind understood its purpose for breath

Is this song that could not rest

Like a path in the desert that keeps going

Of a journey from east to west

Is a heart that when told

Will map out a way to get there

To a willow steady holding

Through a storm that could not best

Are these words from a word God kept

INTERNAL

One   day I fell and watched a dream

Unfolded   peace that sits in me

To   wake not knowing you were sleep

Will   heighten awareness to everything

Apart   from those I was compelled to lean

Ran   to my God to help to help me breathe

Dull   blade still dug out broken piece

"Lord   if not for the grace of thee"

Yesterday   accredited to the shape I keep

TO BEAR

Welcome a season because it must come to pass. Without Fall how would death retain its beauty? Without Winter how would one hibernate to reflect on that season? Without Spring how would the obligation for rebirth play into existence? Each is necessary. Just as Summer break is.

ATMOSPHERE

in a three-story house

each level desolate

top cold as the first

no love to warm them

the land around it dead

only sky showed birth

as rain fell with sunshine

it could only be Him

in that ground nothing grew

dead roots from dying trees

leaning like what it surrounded

eyes return to sky again

no life on that street

sun was just there to rehearse

THE DAYS YOU REMEMBER WILL NEVER RECALL YOU

Strolling in a familiar room

eyes look down or away

In the corner a few turn towards you

Unwittingly, they allow their smirk to tell
more about their state of inebriation

than they try to reveal

A few mock or crack jokes on a previous
circumstance

  that you lack the ability to see the humor in

A square takes you outdoors

Feet finding pavement and your nostrils

the night air,

exhaling slowly, wondering why you even showed
up in the first place

Was it for affirmation

To witness in the flesh that it was over long
before you arrived

or was it to walk away with that smile that
showed up,

 realizing it didn't deserve the energy you
lost

ONE EVENING IN GEORGIA

In the rain just stood

Wondering where you went

As tears fell with them

No one noticed which was which

In truth if they had wouldn't a cared if they
did

Busy day on a crowded street, the drops made
them miss

Although noise around to surround, it was
nothing I'd hear

Pressed on towards chaos and chains that I
invited to let steer

And here the more estranged I became, the
realer the shackles would get

then in dreams I would pack, while those
waiting would disappear,

But those times I noticed your car, I'd take
my time to fill my dear

     I use this image to keep going Grandma.
     My heart. My hero. My air.

DISTANCE MEANS NOTHING

A waste of thought, but seared in ones' mind
with thousands more attached

sitting paused;

do not try to take ahold of what shakes you
off

Will leave you pacing to a drum that didn't
even know you were

and here...

Always accepting less, left to lend what you
cannot afford

And not speaking of currency, but the missing
time

But embrace the height as it's given, for
it's by design

You see all the sun knows is to shine

And like it you will learn of this course

You'll do fine

THOUGHTS TO BURY THIS; TO FLOURISH EACH

tatted canvas

blackened lungs

alcohol for dancing

no rest was won

night would begin in her eyes

so many moons ago

peeling back layers of pride

for grays to settle upon

in the night nothing lives

nothing but gratification

nothing gives

not much holds up of kind

still the protection of Jesus attends

DIFFERENT ROADS

My friends and I ran so very wild

Too smart for a cage, too bold to lie down

That courage had, from bottles passed

Pushed us to build with what we found lying
around

Heart of the south does reside on the sun

The romance of this dance fetched songs some
have sung

A world safe that we made, upheld in that
space

In time we'd grow from all that it was

A demand kept by nature that we grow and
evolve

Enduring our lives, scaling what mountain was
brought

Yesterday. Where it shall remain

My road led to deer and lakes, where snow
shows up in Fall

Where this writer calls home for now...love
returned to you all

ASTONISHING

It can be baffling.

Hard to grasp the concept

At the glow of that which

Has been perfected in the furnace.

Sometimes because it's hard to conceive

The notion we were made that strong and
brilliant

But at the end of the day, could you imagine
a

A Creator that would have sought to make you
otherwise?

SCALING KEYS

A song.

Yes, on this climb you'll fall at times

  The rise is what God cares to mind

A tone. To set a tone

A song.

Just ran to run, because of a need to run

Chasing to piece what felt left undone

But if you'll slow, you'll hear "Be Still"
from home

A song.

Of stars, this look appears out of reach

Christ on throne to say there is no such
thing

  How strong. So very strong

THE HESITATION

Fixing thoughts on you

No Longer shaken or shocked when set on
display

Boldness, this truth

 for doubt made of me a fool

that these words would not form once the
walls fell to lay

Fixing thoughts on you

How to pace in peace like you?

An attempt with this ink

Boldness, this truth

shed light on light, I pray it do

my lord I pray for a beam

fixing thoughts on you

precious act that this heart still moves

as you keep watch over every beat

Boldness, this truth

The footprints the rain washed away

Run no more. To stand All I knows' to do

Boldness, this poet

Boldness, this truth

Fixing thoughts on you

BRAVE IT

fear of some visions, their size and my worth

fear the sword of the tongue, misplaced phrases
misused misunderstood by hurt

fear that my strength is not what it seems

fear fragile mind and hard eyes is too telling
of me

fear every truth that's wrote from each stage

fear that the Spirit will depart from this place
with no trace

hope when I go, to have brought a herd near Him

And hope this weight shows, it is only God that I
fear

SCATTERED

Ever so often a minds' in a place, where it's
fixed on their cross. This expression
intended for patience, a thing without cost.

Everyone is on a different plateau. Some are
dancing now, some are mourning, some are
cracking jokes, some are working, some are
building, some are smiling in the mirror,
some are upset with the mirror, some are
drinking wine, some are searching for water
to drink, some are tired, some are wide
awake.

My sweet Lord, keep us in Your sight

BREADCRUMBS

didn't seek validation

or spoils or rewards

for this life

instead laughter

to wrap souls

this heart knew to recite

if "upholder of the good" is

the title

name bears,

in presence sits

angels

upholding a birthright God prepared

the security still rests

even night when conscious is laid

to know one smiles

one clings

to one line I engraved

EXPOSED

"The night is young!" As it's always been, in a sense. Soon it will be no more, leaving it to have existed as just that. An unbridled youth.

A MOMENT OF SOLACE

Around here quiet it is

 I don't hear a call

With my design to subsist

Dry ink will stage what's been paused

No substance to lift

For Jesus I fall

The sun will kick in

From what I recall

With A chair I declared

That I never saw

 For now, a bed here to rest

Sleep or awake I see God

Left here with poems to give

While shining my guitar

his Spirit resting on me,

Christ illuminating these thoughts

COAT (ARMOR)

mind now clear, this is sure

spirit calm, state is pure

days for work, night to reset

every demon defeated

arrows move quick

vision captures a hill

& strength grown here by God's appeal

commit to smile often

Stand where I choose

So long as that movement upholds my Lord's
will

position a whisper, will still hear it

etched in stone, a command to project,

serenity within, as the rain cleanses still

what loss what gain, the miss the hits

will straighten the path, though narrow it is

this paint on page a guide to His throne

just one to whom we kneel

His breath alone

keeps current moving along

for Christ my King I build

A WATCH AND A KING

My Pa expressed his gratitude for me. For the
man I became,

for the assistance and care I provided in his
hour. In truth, I was only in the position to
do those

things because you always caught me upon
falling. There to reel me back in. It was my
duty and an honor to catch you as you fell.

A fisher of men we be.

STABILITY

Seek God. Seek Him with your whole heart.

SOMETHING, TO STAND ON

This pounding in the chest

Has fell in tune

To only You

These eyes now finding rest

In sleep stay true

Awake am too

These limbs so rarely stressed

By grace we move

By Word we do

This hope not from a guess

Of a boast to choose

remains always you…Elohim

GRACE

Left is what they tell me

Storms fade in my mind

Those seasons He spared me

And now I don't wonder why

Peace erupts in my soul

A light that seems to show

Anchored by angels' role

To ensure my name on His palm

Letting it sink in

 A heartbeat that resounds

I say with a steady tone...

Found

ECHO

Poetry is the quietest way to scream

It doesn't need fancy lines or things to
rhyme

Just truth of what you speak

In this short life lived

Though only short in days, won't count those
nights awake

Learned to yell "Embrace Your Gift!"

RECIPROCAL

Slow to wake the vision kept

To turn to gaze where the sun has crept

Those prayers will ring to ear of my King

Quickly stream from on high till I'm led to
His left

Afraid and yet calm to express His longing of
me

Still I am His servant. My love a fire for He

Though it's nothing I am, that humility a
brand

By faith each request is placed at my feet

Day after day I strive just to be this

A gentle soul that if cold my coat becomes
his

The cover of Christ covers mine, so purely
divine

Strength perfected in my weakness in all that
I'll lift

COUNTRIES

We'll see the sun I say

When the rain that was will pause and wait

And the leaves turn gold in death that day

When the air smells sweet on every stage

And the Fall will scream with its beautiful
death displayed

When the streets are quiet from the noise it
rakes

And wind blows in circles with no thought of
escape

When trees sway to and fro and dare not break

Where birds laugh loud because they know
they're safe

Where all fear comes undone because awareness
gives way

When the coffee and sage give credit to each
for its place

And to simply stand there with a streak of
gray

We'll see the sun I say

MUSIC

think this one will be played by ear

rediscover what's been around since keys

gentle hands finding their shape

across the board, not missing a string

old sounds to embellish

 only miss what's not tried

and these words have a rhythm

each note and lyric I find

you cannot listen and speak

 to notice the lace up of chords

going forward the sound to adhere

melodies to belt out as knees brace the floor

THE OPEN LETTER

A dream of a door that wouldn't lock,

Facing whatever enters

                              Thank you,

my Lord.

PRIORITIES

Heaven above,

in valley our footing we keep.

Each heartbeat alongside

will not vie for first place of worldly
things,

instead a race to a laugh and the closest
beach.

Be Still

Be Strong

Rest on

Press on

Away with Greedy Sharks

Abound in Love Fed

Sunrise Restarts the Clock

To Give Life Another Chance

INVITE

Upheld in a place where the sun shines on me

Upheld by spirits I cannot see

Left here to speak, to fill a sea, start
ankles deep

Left of my God under His wing

MARKINGS OF EGYPT

Just passing a scene, swear I've it seen
before

Embrace it nonchalant as I stay on this
course

And though journey was far as a shot from the
stars

Feel I'm here to help earth spin round once
more

ART

Which musician would I have playing if I only
brought one to listen to, left on an island,

 with no sign of rescue?

Otis Redding. It's the easiest listen. A
sound that I wouldn't tire of.

PRECIPITATION

Something about the rain

Falling free from the sky

Touching things for them to tie

Removing built up pain

There's something about the rain

Makes it easier to breathe

Sun you love, rain you would keep

Left appreciating the frame

Still there's something about the rain

Always promises more

Then each drop it left before

It's worth will be explained

Will always be something comforting about the
rain...

A WRITER

I am a poet I choose no other way

I write what I feel, never feared expression

...or shy away from arrangement

I'm as calm as I appear, I am new as
displayed

I wait patiently for the day to take its
shape

I am a poet I choose no other way

CONTENT

It settled in my heart a while ago

That nothing's desired for the price of my
soul

No dime could shine bright enough to let it
go

No possession that's needed for there are no
holes

No hunger for power no want for control

No need of fame or name to feel whole

No night is too dark nor day that's too long

No harm that could come that would turn it to
stone

I am free.

ON MY WAY

I've come rather far

Some roads can't explain, the knives there
too sharp

Fore' He set Angels surrounding

The bells I did hear, I'll return home when
they draw me

Humble I'll remain

Thoughts of my worth is not for me to trace

SURVIVED TO HOLD YOU...

I remember hugging a young lady after her
aunt had passed. If I could go back to that
moment, I would have held her longer than I
did. Sometimes it's best to let the person
who needed the hug to let go first.

THE MUSIC GRADUATE

I dreamt to find a note to spare

To let the music, share the story

The melody so beautifully prepared

One day hymns will rest on every line I
forward

HOW IT IS

Some days it will just be you, most days.

Embrace this God given strength.

TO BE HONEST

never seen Gone with the Wind, never been
stung by a bee, never went tubbing down a
river, never played the lottery

never been to a Bama game, never finished
first in a race, never kissed a prom queen,
never flown past three hours to a place

never met a blind person from birth, never
slept in the woods, never hiked a mountain,
never sang all that good

never owned a gun, no need when angels by
side, never been this bold in expression,
never felt alone at night

never slept in New York, never mastered the
illusion of cool, never been to a Spanish
country, never called anyone a fool

never built anything from scratch, never
visited Rome, never seen Africa or the Middle
East, never heard most past friends' voice
over the phone

never taken the time to learn to dance with
a woman but slowed once or twice to seek a
wife, Though I've never needed a hand to hold

Even if this letter presumes I might

THE GIANT

few inches smaller but comparing strength… no
one harder

I witnessed this build watched God heal what
they scarred

A few I put there, like yours mine not
visibly shown

I realize there's no need for proof, the
height shows on our souls

While this wandering mind led me down several
streets

That lack of fear there accredited to B

His heart bestowed fitting, the first king in
the flesh that I'd know

And that cross on his chest describes him
best if this don't

Most growth from bro bro who helped clear
this lane

A lion that led with patience and roared
quietly at those that rushed the growth of my
mane

THE BODY

My heart reads my mind

My mind reaches my hands

My hands shake my legs and

My legs start my dance

My dance arrows my back

My back readies my stance

My stance informs my feet

Proclaim to this land,

I am not buried in the ground. It is where I
stand

SILLY BILLY

It's the easiest thing for me to make someone
smile

Usually cause the joke can't be told cause
the laugh is the clown

Silly when a joke is built up then the
punchline is nowhere around

And the harder I try to express it the more
the laughter rolls out

An old colleague said it's a little weird,
especially when the tears start to flow

I say it's been that way since the late 80's,
the delivery about the same tone, as 3
decades had noticed

SHORT STORY

Visions arose in my youth, many to hold
or to reach. Of soft rain there to hug,
beauty's what inspired me. I walked down
hills and pass

fields through creeks and streams. Often
carrying a notebook not believing this is
what I'd be. In Center Point I believed that
my job was to

dream. A child in a house filled with books,
and musicians in headphones to teach. My
youth saw such things like high sun and the
beach.

Though the beach was a lake and that sun
never ceased. All the while taking note of
Langston Hughes & Maya Angelou and Mrs.
Lindsey my

6th grade teacher. Influenced by soft rock
and those Motown kings. Daddy's side
delivered Marvin, so Mama Bear brought Anita.
My Nannah

blasted Soft Rock 94.5 in hopes to win the
lottery. Produced my love for Faith, Phil and

Elton along with Ben E. King. Meemaw loved hard on

Labelle for me not would have been treason. I grew to love artists and poetry and the tune I hear beneath them. My respect is of a craft that

 keeps man common with each. The art of poetry, music, expression is the best I believe. My courage rests in this pen, my strength in its ink.

My guitar's name is Uma, that is strummed as needed.

EVERY YEAR IN NOVEMBER

Every year on return how another seed's sown

For every worry I put away, things start to
heal on their own

This time of year, I feel the earth to wind
down

And the air around quiet, as the land is
chill now

Each birthday grows this heart, as more
strength will abound

ENCOURAGE

If you gather yourself to rise before the sun
yawns again

Several angels are present. Thousands of
hands

If you lack bread or a place to lie safe

It is just for a moment. Even if years it's a
day

If your heart fills with grief for a love
that you lost

Heaven holds the faithful departed. To speak
is to call

If your limbs have gone numb cause they're
forever in motion

Know peace will one day surround everything
that beholds Him

PEANUT M&M'S FOR MOM

Some say I've grown into the humblest of men

If limbs sang their own song

My Mother could hum every hymn

In college then to work, prepare a meal then
head lost in her books

Never recall complaining

Just singing Brownstone and Sam Cooke

Kept her children cultured with novels,
museums and art

Keeps us ensured

We're treasure she'd never part

Her prayers sit powerful and quiet her tone

Her gaze can start wars

But calm to us cause its home

Thank you for the chapters

I will live on Mama Bear

No more breaking or falling and no more tears

...only laughter and peace in abundance Ma

1:23 AM

A couple notice me

A few stay close to me

And some stay woke for me

There're the ones holding me

There're those that pray for me

As this is shaping me

For every page it brings

Here's love to you from me

These thoughts they rush to me

Hours where it's just me

Of all that's made of me

Walk talk stand differently

Cause in the end you see

No boasting heard from me

Yet know that purposely

Silent work will rock the sea

A NOTICE TO ROSES

guard heart as you go

but teach what lesson was loaned

hear, and learn

pray, and serve

feel what you lose

then paint as you move

share what is earned

live like your turn

remove what is broke

cry and then don't

love, do it bold

attest spirit's gold

see, and embrace

dream, and then chase

heal more, in time

and help heal those you find

MY DUTY

I don't pretend to know all or understand

Or question my Father's will

Of how in fire the flame never overcame

Or that lift on a cloud

To rest then return with a pen He gave

With saints and angels surrounding this man

My Lord, the strength that vision engraved

Fought to express these words this way

BEAT NEVER STOPS

Music lays within my dreams

Songs I've never heard

I wake to tunes that stay with me

But never remember words

The groove what I embrace the most

The melody is what remains

I am just a chord a note

In a key I could not name

LIT

The heart of you sat new to me

One of the kindest ones, why most will lean

Don't take it for granted or let hurt brand
it

Nor allow it to harden from anything

To keep you shielded as your grass remains
green

Your eyes' your gift of how you see

When you paint life's passage

Take what growth those images bring

On every continent you'll shake the tree

For fruit to fall on the earth beneath

What you'll ignite with a brush

Is a conversation they hushed

Use every color, as you're made of each

Know your worth, know your reach

And remember when a crystal reflects light
off the moon and stars at night

Darkness gets lit up forever to be

LONERS PERSPECTIVE

There will be days you loath it and days
you'll own it

It's the most complex emotion I think

It will make you question yourself as an
individual

Did I choose this, or did it seek me out?

It can make you strong, bold and confident in
your own skin

Yet it's able to make you doubt life and
love, things sometimes you feel you take no
part in

It can force you to see a light in everyone's
eyes from their stories, no matter how simple
or extravagant

Goodness gracious...it can even let you
imagine yourself to have taken part in them

It allows you to dream, to breathe, to reach
for whatever you desire

Allows time to speak to God. Holy curiosity,
I've heard it called.

It sets you apart,

Stands you up

It's why I laugh, because it taught me who I
am...

VAULT

I will never confine someone to remain in my presence

It has never been in my nature to force someone into a place they no longer have a desire to be.

I graciously move to establish companionship, and a mutual respect between us,

And if at any point they wish to depart, my reply is, "be well." And just because there's no memorabilia I hold to,

does not mean anything. The pictures, notes, tips and laughs remain in the strongest safekeep I own…TIAM

It's never too late in the day to decide to do good. Most will say "the cards are stacked against me or I'm too far gone."

This is the false narrative satan wants you to believe. It's too late for it. Man becomes blind by the snares it

Tries to set in front of us, though my Lord Jesus spoke, no weapon formed against thee shall prosper.

Let the wicked become entangled in their own traps, as this will always be the case when you attempt to rise against God's elect.

(UN) TIED

Broken away from the women I never had

Belonging to no one to this I am latched

I hold to this truth

Heartache causes relapse

To a forest I've already been

Shores of Spain now where head's at

Still recall the beauty they projected

In parting this writer with passion

INSIDE (SIGH)

It came to my attention

on my last go round',

that the moon was a light I had grown

accustomed to, as the stars guided those
nights.

So, if you see me squinting or looking down
nowadays, it's because I'm

getting used to the daylight.

Although foreign, it is preferable.

(LABELED) ARTISTIC

Jesus overcoming death I sit now as God's
servant Christ's freeman

Road embraced as was given, was daunting yet
still left believing

As some understand the road of repetition
allows for actions to be consistent

The guide from these saints and these angels
allowed me to keep this

calm in a quiet state

like the Spirit set on this man

Nothing troubled nor storm could shake

It is Christ who strengthens these hands

Resting on heaven's gate

A decree I'll prepare for The Potter to brand

To remove the wicked and cast away

Left to walk with Him, in awe of God with
each glance

MIND (SET)

Word.smith: /werdsmiTH/

    noun

a skilled user of words

...write on

About the Author

Born in Detroit, Michigan in 85' and raised in Birmingham, Alabama in the 90's, during what some would consider a peaceful era in America. Darius E. Scaife spent his days listening to past present and upcoming artists of all genres, along with traveling to downtown Birmingham to attend an institute that taught young students writing and different rhyming techniques in poetry. Having been raised in a single parent household with his Mother, a graduate from the University of Alabama at Birmingham, and older brother, he was taught the importance of being there for others and the appreciation of those who have been there for you. She shared with him her love of music, art, literature and to always use his right to freedom of speech. Having left high school before 11th grade he went back to obtain his GED and would go on to graduate from the online program at Full Sail University with a Bachelor of Science in Music Business. During his life he endured many self-inflicted hardships and unforeseen life tragedies he would overcome through his love of poetry, music and faith in God. His love for writing continues today. He is currently enrolled at Southern New Hampshire University and is studying English and Creative Writing w/c Poetry.

Made in the USA
Middletown, DE
08 September 2020